You Missed A Spot:

We're Diverse, I'm Inclusive

K. AGIRI

You Missed A Spot:
We're Diverse, I'm Inclusive
by K. Agiri

ISBN paperback: 978-1-5272-3604-2
ISBN ebook: 978-1-5272-3597-7

Published by Agiri Publishing

Cover design by Bola Lasisi-Agiri.
Interior design by Manos Design.

71-75 Shelton Street
Covent Garden
London, United Kingdom
WC2H 9JQ

Ymasbook@gmail.com

Instagram: @YMASBook

CONTENTS

Preface

Quick question for you: have you ever had an *unpleasant* thought and then tried quickly to forget it, but you *can't*? It's done. You've clocked on and now you can't clock out and get the thought out of your mind.

You know those times when you just stare into space for a couple of seconds as you play out the thought, before you can snap back to reality. I had one of those moments about eight years ago. Yet for some reason this particular thought wasn't as easy as others to shrug off.

I've now come to the conclusion that the thought wasn't supposed to be forgotten. It needed to be addressed face-on, potentially helping others in the process. As you read on, the unpleasant thought that I had might resonate with you. Or, it might be something that's never crossed your mind. Either way, I hope you will appreciate the heads-up that this book aims to provide.

"You Missed A Spot: We're Diverse, I'm Inclusive" is essentially the birth child of:

1. An unpleasant thought that I first had roughly eight years ago

2. My experiences from the time I started university in 2010 through to the initial years of my professional career

3. Meaningful conversations that I've had with my closest friends

It would probably help if I told you what the unpleasant thought was, so here you go:

Although I've always counted myself as a well-rounded and well-informed person, when I got to university and made new friends, and then again when I began my career in the world of finance, I felt as though I knew next to nothing about so many things. Things that my peers all seemed to be interested in.

Realising there was a gap in my knowledge was one thing to deal with, but the thought of how obvious this gap was to my friends and colleagues was even scarier.

It made me wonder if my lack of awareness about certain sports, travel experiences, certain forms of art and culture, hobbies, interests, and fine dining might pose a bigger problem for me in the future?

Introduction

Nowadays, some of the most esteemed educational institutions and big corporations across a range of industries are finally shaking up their admissions policies and processes. Better late than never!

They are opening up to the idea of accepting candidates from different backgrounds to their usual picks. Whether or not they are kickstarting these initiatives for the right reasons is an important question, but one for another time, but to cut a long story short, we are moving toward a better place when it comes to diversity and inclusion in the corporate world.

However, from my own experiences, and also from speaking to others, it's clear that there is a problem being ignored here. What happens to candidates like me who get propelled into these understandably unfamiliar territories and realise that our race, religion, or creed is in fact *not* the most significant difference between us and nearly everyone else around us? What about the differences in social backgrounds, which inevitably lead to very different tastes, hobbies and interests?

You might ask:

But does that really matter?

The answer is, yes. In an ideal world, everyone would have equal and seamless access to and knowledge of all that's good on the planet. In a perfect world, you would already be fully in-tune with everything that supports your growth and potentially your career development. And in a different world, your tastes, interests and hobbies would be all be refined tastes, interests and hobbies. They'd also be clear signs of prestige and the fact that you were brought up well.

Well, I'm sorry to have to break it to you...We don't live in an ideal or perfect world. For reasons I will come to in a little while, there's a fair chance that you've missed the memos that many of your peers have received throughout their lives.

That's not to say that your tastes, hobbies and interests are inferior to the ones that I will talk about in this book, rather that it pays to know more. The wider your knowledge base, and the broader your perspective, the better.

So are you saying that I need to be more like my colleagues to progress?

Nope. I genuinely believe that we can only reach our highest potential by being the best version of ourselves. You're not going to read this book and decide you need to start over in life. You've obviously done something right to get to where you are today and hopefully this book will support your future progress in one way or another.

The key thing to note here is that being yourself doesn't have to mean you put up a fence against or, worse, a middle finger to everything else. Take pride in your ability to be versatile and open to new things that can benefit you in important ways.

But isn't the whole idea of diversity and inclusion about encouraging people from different backgrounds to mix?

Some might say yes, but I don't think that's the whole story. The initial step of bringing together people from different backgrounds is just that, an initial step. What's also important is for all of these people to feel like they belong, and the effective sharing of information and best practices.

It's not about embracing the hobbies, interests or culture of your peers just so that they like you more. Even if I think common ground does help to form quality relationships, that's not the most important thing here. What's most important is you being the most open-minded version of you; that way, you can make informed decisions about whether something really is or isn't for you.

Surely if these things were actually beneficial to me, I would already know about them?

Sadly, this isn't necessarily the case. There are three over-arching reasons why you might not be a fountain of knowledge when it comes to the things I will highlight in this book:

1. Cost – More often than not, the monetary price we must pay in order to play dictates our experiences. Some of the activities I will cover are traditionally pretty expensive to get involved with, and that's understandably been a barrier to access. Don't worry, though, I'll be highlighting a few pocket-friendly ways to proceed.

2. Exclusivity – This often goes hand in hand with high prices, but not always. Some of the things I will mention have historically been reserved for people from certain backgrounds and social status's.

The good news is that times are changing, and for the better. Social media is helping to put the spotlight on discriminators and inclusive alternatives are being formed and rightly favoured.

3. Environment – We're all products of our environments in one way or another. It's easier to take an interest in what's around you than things you only see or hear of once in a blue moon. Previously you may have dismissed some of the things in this book maybe as 'too bourgeois', perhaps 'too boring', or you may not have even considered some of them at all. That's fine. Let's see if this book can help you to make more informed decisions.

I'm going to assume that you're all good with the whole 'you need to work hard' part of the equation when it comes to your career success. If not, I'm sorry but you're not going to get that from me here.

This book will support the hard work you're already doing and provide you with a fresh perspective on a wide range of topics, including sports, travel, arts and culture, hobbies and interests, and fine dining. You'd need to be an absolute machine to take on everything that I detail in this book but if that's you, do your thing!

The topics I will discuss are the areas where I've noticed the greatest dissimilarities that I believe stem directly from differences in social class and upbringing. However, I wouldn't be surprised if there are more areas to touch on another time. To fully embrace the key messages of this book, you'll need to read on with an open mind.

If you've just started working in the corporate world, this book is for you. Or, you might already have some experience of working in the corporate setting —no worries, this book is for you, too. Even if you're not currently working in a corporate role but simply want to be enlightened, guess what… this book is also for you!

Some of this might go over your head, some of it might not be for you and some of this might not be easy to swallow. That's fine, receiving the information is the key thing. Whether you then go on to use this book to help you plan things to do over weekend, or to connect and socialise with your peers a bit more, is totally up to you!

Let's focus on the part of the diversity and inclusion equation that we can control and action now – investing in ourselves! Whether it's a big or small investment is not important at this stage.

Then, it's for all parties to prove just how open, unassuming and inquisitive they really are. This book will help you make the first move and set an example in the journey toward genuine diversity and inclusion.

Why Did I Write This Book?

I decided to bring the idea for this book to life after a meeting with my mentor and close friend. I want to make it clear that writing this book wasn't a long-term goal or vision of mine. The plan has always been to help others out once I was in a position to do so, but doing so in the form of a book was a very quick, 'start and don't look back' kind of decision. It feels weird to refer to myself as an 'author'. To be honest, I rarely even read books anymore…

Of course, growing up, I had to get through the set books that formed part of the school curriculum. And then I had a spell when I was 21 or so where all of a sudden I got back into reading, getting through about eight books in as many weeks. What I'm trying to say is that I didn't get to this point now because of some everlasting love for books, reading or writing, but from a recognition of how important it is to share useful information.

Who said money makes the world go round? I'd argue that it's information that makes the world go round! That's probably why, when something catches my interest, I'll go online and read up on it, watch a couple of YouTube videos, or scan through my socials for the latest info.

I value the power that's associated with being in the know and in possession of useful information, but also the all-important next step of sharing that information. This book gives me the chance to impart what I believe is useful information to people who can benefit from it.

This was my primary motivation for writing this book!

It was also a nice way to connect with old friends and acquaintances. I decided to conduct some primary research in the form of a ten-question survey on *hobbies and interests* to see whether my assumptions, outlined in the previous chapter, were correct. By the end, I had collected just over 100 survey responses from people who I went to school or college with and a couple more from people who I randomly met on my recent local travels around the capital.

Throughout the book, I'll be sharing the results of the questionnaire with you.

Author's Journey

In terms of who I am, I want you to imagine the charisma of Denzel Washington, mixed with the presence of Idris Elba, and the humour of Will Smith. Or…

You can take the more accurate description and imagine a 27-year-old black British male. Someone born and raised in Southeast London, now with over four years' experience in a relatively rewarding investment management sales role.

I'm not a disconnected scholar with loads of fancy letters at the end of my name because I've spent my whole life reading on the topic of diversity and inclusion, or decades cramped up in an office analysing and producing academic research.

I'm someone who can relate to the topic of diversity and inclusion based on real-life experience. I'm someone who's done his homework and is not a fan of a lot of the half-hearted, all talk and no action contributions to the discussion.

I view being a first-generation Brit raised by Nigerian parents to be a huge plus. My parents simultaneously reinforced two somewhat contrasting but equally important messages when I was growing up:

1. Self-worth – I was regularly reminded to hold onto this at all times and to remember that I was destined for great things, so there was no need to exhibit fear or be doubtful.

2. Underdog spirit – My dad repeatedly stated that I had to be prepared to work twice as hard as some of my peers in order to succeed. I assumed that this was because of our race more than anything else.

Some might find this top dog/underdog duality confusing, but the feeling of being both privileged and disadvantaged at the same time was something that inspired me, and still does.

The route I took to get to where I am today was not conventional, but I'm not complaining…

Early years

Throughout my entire educational journey I attended state schools. In primary school, I was one of quite a few kids from African households but there was a real mix of students from other nationalities to form ties with. Where your parents came from was rarely ever the deciding factor behind who you chilled with; it was more about tastes and interests, and how well-behaved or naughty you were.

Early teens

Even though my secondary school was a public school it was one of the most well-regarded schools in the local area. You had to take an aptitude test as part of your application and there was a strict catchment area.

I would say the school had around a 70/30 split in terms of white students to Black, Asian and Minority Ethnic (BAME) students. But race wasn't a big thing to take notice of in school — at least, it wasn't really something that prevented relationships from forming.

Late teens

Later, in college, the racial split between black people versus all other races was more or less 80/20, so I definitely wasn't part of a minority.

However, a handful of my close friends and I made a bit of a name for ourselves in college. Nearly all of us were able to buy our own cars before our 18th birthdays (which wasn't too common) and all of us had decent-paying retail jobs. That meant that we had enough to waste money on clothes and trainers with little fuss, and enough to treat some girls to a Nando's.

University

This was the first time in my life where it was a challenge to spot anyone with my skin colour. Whilst that was strange, it was also quite funny to me, and something I'd tell all my friends and family at home about whenever we caught up. To be honest I didn't even need to tell them… They'd tell me, after they'd seen the Facebook pictures I'd be tagged in from nights out.

Being one of the few black people in sight was interesting, but it was the underlying differences in views, tastes and interests that really struck me. I'd made new friends pretty quickly, and knew a diverse set of people. Irrespective of race, the main takeaway from my university experience was that a lot of people came from what sounded like affluent, privileged backgrounds.

Even though a lot of my friends didn't really know each other before university, they somehow all seemed to have similar knowledge of things outside of uni that I wasn't really aware of, and hadn't been exposed to. It was more this than my race that made me an oddball, but it wasn't something to dwell on.

What did bother me was the stigma that I felt people attached to where I was from. Fair enough, Southeast London is not known for being all sunshine and roses, but I didn't know the perception was as bad as it was until I began to meet more people at university.

I remember having a nice chat with a girl who I met through one of my uni friends. She was from a small town in Hampshire and our mutual friend was from Windsor, so they weren't a million miles apart from each other back home. The next day, he let me know that she had been shocked at how nice I was considering the fact that I came from "such a rough background."

To this day I find this funny – we didn't speak about our backgrounds at all.

I spent the next few years at university meeting new people and converting negative preconceptions into more positive opinions of what a black person from South London was like.

Premature judgment wasn't a new concept to me but university reaffirmed that we are all guilty of this, and that the most important thing I could do was to be open-minded and the truest version of myself.

Corporate World

In many respects, university was a taster course for what was to come in the world of work. By this I mean that I came from a fairly different background to most of the people who I would be surrounded by in my chosen profession.

Thankfully, my experience in the corporate world kicked off pretty much straight after I wrapped up my final year exams. The stars aligned for me when I landed my dream first job on a fund sales desk at a large investment management company. Five years on, at the time of writing, I'm still firmly placed in the same industry, working in my dream role at a large European investment firm.

However, in the five years that have passed I've not been able to completely shake off that unpleasant thought. I've spoken to others in my industry and friends working within other corporate sectors and it seems like my unpleasant thought has been shared by far more people than I first imagined.

In my search for a wider base of knowledge and experience in regard to certain sports, travel, art, hobbies and interests, and fine dining, it hit me that there are a lot of good things out there that I had been, and perhaps you are, disconnected from, whether intentionally or unintentionally.

Hopefully sharing this useful information will be the first step in bridging that gap.

Enjoy!

Chapter One – Sports

So, how was your weekend?

The sanctity of the weekend magnifies when you're working in the corporate world. The weekend is your conversation starter on a Friday, and likewise on a Monday.

You ask almost anyone you work with "how was your weekend?" or if they "have any plans for the weekend ahead?" and almost instantly, you're in the land of close ties. If you manage to find a common thread between your plans and theirs, you'd better watch they don't ask you to marry them! Okay, that's a slight exaggeration, but you get the point.

My first full-time job was on a sales desk that was dominated by men, and this question would more often than not lead to discussions about sport. *What did you watch? What did you play?*

What I noticed pretty quickly was that my knowledge of sport centred around just two sports: football and boxing. Whenever rugby, cricket, golf, formula one and, to some extent, tennis came into the mix, I'd eject myself from the conversation.

That was my reality, though I can appreciate that sport may not come up in conversation for you as much as it did for me. Either way, for reasons I will come to in this chapter, a broad appreciation for sport can pay dividends in conversation as well as support you physically, helping you stay fit and healthy. Hopefully, there will be something for everyone in this chapter.

I took a step back and consciously explored the reasons behind my concentrated knowledge when it came to following and participating in sport.

The simple answer would have been that I preferred to follow sports that I personally enjoyed playing. But I've never stepped foot in a boxing gym; my delicate nose and I have never competed in any form of sparring match.

For me, the truth was that there were simply some sports that the people around me and I would speak about or play, and others that we didn't. This was reflected in the sports I would watch and the sportspeople who I looked up to, the likes of Thierry Henry or Mike Tyson. My knowledge of other sportspeople was limited to only a handful of the major superstars in other sports. Don't get me wrong, I knew of Brian Lara, Serena Williams, Lewis Hamilton and, of course, Tiger Woods. Notice a pattern?

My Limited Interest vs Limited Exposure

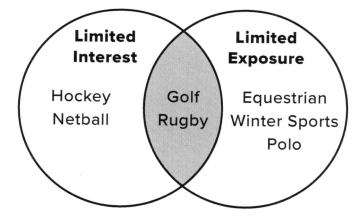

As an industry, sport has an amazing ability to bring people together, similar to the music industry. It's not about selecting one kind of people over another, but rather a powerful tool to connect people from different walks of life.

However, if you drill down a bit deeper, there are some sports that truly are watched, played and loved by people from a wide mix of backgrounds, and others where I'm not so sure that this is the case.

Some of these sports are arguably only inclusive if you fit the bill, and implicit barriers make it harder for others to take an interest and get stuck in to the same extent. For me, golf is an example of such a sport.

In defence of the beautiful thing that is sport, in some cases it is simply a matter of people using sport in a deliberately divisive way. I'm almost certain that some people follow particular sports because of the prestige and connotations that are associated with it, and judge others if they're not similarly tuned in.

I'd be lying if I said it surprised me when a couple of privileged girls from my university told me that they'd never date a guy who played in the football team, yet they adored every member of the rugby team and the golf team. With sport comes symbolism; it can be a tool to help distinguish between one breed of person and another, but I'd rather use it to help build bridges not walls.

As we move toward a more inclusive environment in education and professional services, I see certain sports becoming more mainstream and accessible to all. We're already seeing this with golf. Nowadays, for less than £20 you can hire out some golf clubs and balls and vibe with your friends (or date) at a TopGolf venue.

It's also cool to see more people embracing sports like boxing, whether it's through coming together to support homegrown talent like Anthony Joshua and Tyson Fury, or actually getting involved yourself, for example in increasingly popular corporate challenges like white collar boxing. This is one of my favourite examples of how sport can really bring people from different walks of life together.

One of the questions I asked in my questionnaire was:

If one sport could remain, both in terms of watching and playing, which sport would you choose?

Boxing 39%
Cricket 3%
Golf 9%
Formula One 7%
Rugby 5%
Tennis 37%

Just in case you were wondering how I could forget football... I didn't!

I'm almost certain football would have been the top choice for most respondents, given that it is the most popular sport in the world by a country mile. But this fact actually makes it less important in the context of this book.

My results highlighted boxing as the top answer, which wasn't a surprise. But I was surprised there wasn't an overly strong dominance in the number of people that chose boxing. This suggests that perhaps there is more interest in a wider variety of sports outside of football than I had originally imagined.

Another interesting takeaway was that all of the respondents who voted for rugby were white. I am sure there's an underlying reason for this but I'd rather not jump to any conclusions on this finding.

One thing I do know is that some sports are indisputably more expensive to play than others. Whether it's the prices of the facilities, such as golf course membership fees, or the cost of actually buying all the gear, getting involved often isn't cheap.

If you have ever studied anything related to business and economics, you probably will have come across the phrase 'barriers to entry', which are essentially obstacles that are likely to make it a challenge for new participants to get involved in something being done by others already. The price to play certain sports is a barrier to entry.

The sports that you're exposed to at school play a big part in shaping your interests. As I said earlier, my secondary school was one of the better ones in the area so we did play other sports, like hockey, but it definitely felt like a slapdash slot-filler in our curriculum. We'd play it for, say, half a term and typically that would almost always be the term when our PE teacher was away so we'd end up playing football anyway. I guess that was because it was easier for the supply teacher to manage, and what we wanted to play most.

A former England cricketer called Ed Smith highlighted some issues with the links between sports and social class in his book *Luck: What It Means and Why It Matters*[1]. The fact that many state schools simply can't afford to get their kids involved in the sports that later down the line help candidates distinguish themselves against their peers is a shame at the minimum.

The problem highlighted in this chapter is simple: social class generally dictates the sports that people will play and follow, and this can have adverse effects on people from working class backgrounds when mixing with people from middle and upper class backgrounds. Solutions to plug the gaps in access to particular sports are trickling in, but more needs to be done here. The following is some information relating to some of the most prestigious popular sports:

INFORMATION

Golf

● The 'Business Sport': my mentor told me years ago that "business often gets firmed up on a golf course.". It's a nice way to spend a healthy amount of time away with your clients and converse about relevant topics in between playing time.

● Read between the lines: golf is played globally but it has a British essence to it in terms of the amount of unspoken rules that you're expected to just know, whether these are what you should wear, what you should say, or how you should conduct yourself on a course. Examples include always wearing a collared shirt on the course.

- Kudos: you can quickly establish yourself in a conversation if you've played at some of the most prestigious courses or have a nice and tidy low handicap.

- Timeless: golf is definitely a sport you can keep playing right through to retirement and beyond, so that should be some comfort for late joiners.

- Loads of small wins = big wins: providing you can get down to a driving range regularly, it's one of those sports that you can keep chipping away at (no pun intended) and fine tune your development over time. Twilight sessions (afternoon-evening) are the cheaper slots to book, as you don't get a full day of sun.

● Related advantages: individual skill and discipline shine through but the sport still encourages good sportsmanship. This sportsmanship is even extended to what's expected of the audience. Professional golfers usually require nearby spectators to be quiet as they putt or hit.

Rugby

● A sociable affair: in London at least, there's a real middle-upper class ring to "spending a day out at the rugby… Or at least national team rugby. Even those who don't religiously follow the sport may say they enjoy a day out at Twickenham. There's usually lots of drinking involved and raised spirits all round, despite the brutal nature of the sport and regardless of the end result.

● Difficult for schools: public schools rarely include rugby in their curricula, but private schools love it. There are always red flags being waved highlighting the physical dangers of tackling in the sport.

- Watch and enjoy: rugby is definitely an exciting sport to watch or play if you're into it, but it's nowhere near as favoured as football. It probably won't cost you the shirt off your back to watch your local team play – that is, if you have a local team.

- Get behind your country: the international team are generally more well-regarded by fans than our national football team players are by footy fans. As the sport is not as widely marketed or televised as football, rugby players are not paid as much as their footballing counterparts. However, the players are certainly better rewarded in terms of respect from supporters.

- Participate: if you're ever considering playing socially but are concerned about safety, there's a modified way to get involved, known as tag rugby. This is a non-contact version of the sport, and also a favourite for corporate challenges. However, if you want to play the uncensored, purest version of the game, there are local clubs in the 'nicer' parts of the capital. One reason for this is that the 'not so nice' parts of London don't have a lot of greenery.

Tennis

● Good watch: it's almost impossible to not appreciate the significance of speed when you're watching or playing tennis. As a tennis player, hand-eye coordination is your best friend.

● Superstars: tennis has produced a whole host of individual superstars with huge followings, and equally huge pay cheques for those regarded as the best in the business. For me, what's unique about a sport like tennis is the fact that both male and female players have arguably been shot up to equal heights of stardom, and gender inequality is cited as a much bigger issue in other sports.

● Major tournaments ('Grand Slams'): are highly regarded tournaments and there usually aren't enough tickets to satisfy the amount of people keen to watch it live. Tennis is one of those sports where people with little interest in the sport will still attend the games because of what they symbolise.

● Classy affair: there is a prescribed level of etiquette that has to be respected on the court. Silence, or at least very little commotion, is expected from the crowd during play. The class dynamics really hit home for me when I heard that Lewis Hamilton was denied entry into Wimbledon's Royal Box because he wasn't wearing a tie or blazer.

● Social watch: tennis is associated with good weather, a pair of Ray Bans, and Pimm's on ice. If you miss out on tickets you can still head out to SW15 for a view of the matches from Wimbledon Common.

- Wrapped up in luxury: whilst tennis doesn't necessarily have to be an expensive sport to play, courts are often situated in quiet and exclusive country clubs and therefore associated with the luxury prices of spa retreats, with their saunas and hot tubs. There are certainly cheaper sports options out there, that lack some of the fancy frills.

- Proud history: this is another homegrown sport, so there's a heritage by virtue and we've developed some of the best players to grace the professional world stage. Names such as Fred Perry, Sue Barker, and Andy Murray are all up there!

- Courts are dotted across the capital so in principle it's not too hard to get involved. Tennis may be prestigious in nature but it's a fairly straightforward, fun sport that I'd personally recommend to everyone.

It's a great way to stay fit and have fun while playing.

There is a whole family of racquet sports: tennis, table tennis, badminton and squash. They are all sociable options to get involved in and boost your overall fitness at the same time.

Cricket

● Social watch: Cricket is one of the sports where it's common to see a whole flow of children, parents and grandparents turning out to watch their favourite team. Fans tend to love the atmosphere because the lengthy games and frequent breaks make it possible to socialise with other spectators without missing any action. If you like a beer, there's a good chance you'll enjoy the atmosphere at a cricket match!

● Local reach: a major sporting ground like the Oval is easy enough to get to and tickets are often relatively cheap. There are also a number of cricket clubs dotted across the capital, which makes playing with others pretty easy. However, the cost of the equipment you need to play isn't a particularly accommodating aspect of the sport.

- Multi-dimensional: a sport that encourages teamwork and is also heavily reliant on individual discipline throughout games. As cricket matches are usually played across several days some find the sport boring, but if you follow it you'll definitely want to stay updated with the latest news of who's batting and who's scored what.

- Questionable inclusion at the top: there's historically been a disproportionate number of players who went to public schools representing the England national team.

- A significant history: the sport was born out of British aristocracy and spread globally throughout the colonial rule of the British

Empire. Hence, it's a prized sport amongst the nations of the Commonwealth.

Field Hockey

● Pay-up: field hockey is arguably one of the least inclusive sports, simply because the cost of purchasing the equipment needed to play can add up to substantial amounts. And that's before you even get into the usual price premiums added on top for the most popular brands. It's not cheap for adults, and it's not cheap for state schools to teach, unless they've got significant spending power.

● Team camaraderie: this is almost a given within this sport, which makes it an effective means to meet people from particular backgrounds. Like its 11-a-side cousin, football and hockey teams are dotted across the capital but there are nowhere near as many to get involved with.

● Gender equity: like tennis, both male and female players play the sport from a young age and receive their fair dues of acclamation.

● Limited reach: perhaps it's the cost of procuring hockey equipment, or maybe it's the lack of exposure at the grassroots level, but field hockey isn't a big-hitting sport outside of middle-upper class circles. It's a strange one, considering it is an Olympic sport.

Formula One

● To go or not to go: if you're watching the championships from the comfort of your home then Formula One is an easy sport to follow, but the stage is truly international, so if you're thinking about going out to watch the street race at the Grand Prix in Monaco or the Championships race in Abu Dhabi, be prepared to part with some cash. When you factor in ticket prices, flights and accommodation, the total cost racks up.

- Individual skill: Lewis Hamilton has certainly reintroduced stardom to the British racing world and has put F1 on the map amongst a younger crowd. He's got the sort of hold on the sport that Michael Schumacher had in his heyday.

- Fun for everyone: karting is a lively sport to get involved in and it stimulates a bit of healthy competition. There are a handful of racing tracks dotted across the city with perks tied to memberships and group bookings.

Chapter Two – Travel

Go hard or go on holiday

You say tomato, I say tomato. You say holiday and I say… headache.

Not travelling too often while growing up made me lose sight of the importance of some time off. That and my stubborn nature. Wanting to get things done had me believing it was okay to work all year round with very little in the way of genuine time off of work. In my mind, travelling was just one of those things on your to-do list that you always say you'll come back to but never get round to actually doing.

But it wasn't that I just *forgot* to travel. I just didn't see the importance of taking scheduled breaks when I wasn't a) rich, or b) indispensable in my job. The "Go hard or go home" attitude wasn't necessarily a problem, but my lack of appreciation of the importance of a pit-stop definitely was.

When I started my career, I didn't have a bank of holiday memories to share, like many of my peers, and the fact my family holidays were limited to trips "back home," to me, really wasn't a big deal... At least not until I got into the working world, where it hit me like a tonne of bricks just how big a deal it was!

In 2012 I was matched up with an industry mentor through a programme that linked young people from inner London with employees who worked for one of the world's largest investment managers. One of the first and best things I did with my mentor was a goal-setting exercise, where I had to come up with some short-term (less than one year), medium-term (3-5 years), and long-term goals (5+ years). I put down "travel more often" as a goal for the long term and my mentor persuaded me to change it to a short to medium-term goal... I understand now why he did that.

For me, the advantages of travelling outweigh the costs by a mile, provided you do it right and start being intentional with it. Don't get me wrong, it's not as deep as having to set goals and objectives for each holiday you go on, but you should have some idea of why you're travelling. Ideally, your holiday should involve some time away from the people who you're around day in, day out. So, whilst I get the logic of travelling abroad because a lot of people you know are going, that shouldn't be your sole motivation to travel.

Just like the smart devices we put in our pockets or carry in our bags nowadays, we also need to recharge ourselves at some point in order to get back to 100%, and an official 'break' is a good way to do this. Whilst you could rightly argue that you don't necessarily have to get away to recharge, I see little reason why you wouldn't, when it's possible.

We'll come to where you can go a bit later, but the point I'm making here is to go. Get away from your usual routine, go with friends or go alone. It might be a well-planned break with plenty of notice, or a spontaneous breakaway. Regardless, the point is to jet off and really appreciate recharging yourself.

A recharge break doesn't have to be a beach holiday, and it doesn't necessarily have to be outside of the country. One of the biggest things I noticed when I got to university, and later when I spoke to colleagues at work, was how little I appreciated the rest of the country outside London.

I had friends in university who had only seen a few black people in their hometowns, which intrigued me – I wanted to find out where the hell they lived, and how this was possible! According to the Office of National Statistics[2] Census data for 2011, "86% of all people in England and Wales were from white ethnic groups."

It's easy to lose sight of this reality when you're born and raised in London. A good way to build on your knowledge of the UK would be to get out and visit the UK, a little excursion here and there might pay well.

Recent stats published by the Department for Transport [3] highlighted that "black people travelled the smallest distance and made the fewest trips compared to other races in the UK." This is a stat that sadly doesn't surprise me at all, but it's definitely a relatively inexpensive fix once the desire to travel is there.

I definitely get it because, in the nicest way possible, I didn't give a hoot about most of the places that my colleagues seemed to be in awe over. Not based on their descriptions, anyway. In my mind, it must have been a race thing, or even an age thing, but I was almost certain that these places weren't going to be for me anytime soon.

It was only when I eventually decided to find out

what all the fuss was about that my appreciation began to form. It makes a difference to go out and find out first-hand why certain places in the UK are officially Areas of Outstanding Natural Beauty. I started to clock on to why my colleagues were so excited about the long weekends where they'd leave straight from the office and head over to places like the Cotswolds or other areas in the countryside.

Let me keep it one hundred with you; there are some UK excursion destinations that people rant and rave about that I genuinely think are just hype, but there's nothing wrong with finding out for yourself. Worst-case scenario, it's crap, you come back, but at least you can spend some of that cultural capital and share your experiences in conversation.

Next up on the list of reasons to travel is a phrase you hear people use all the time and, as cliché as it might sound, travelling really does help you to "expand your horizons." This is one of the greatest advantages that people who are well travelled have over their counterparts without that first-hand experience.

I personally know some people who come from relatively comfortable backgrounds who have decided to fly out to some less than comfortable destinations for no other reason than to enhance their appreciation of what they have. It might have started off with a simple thought like, "I wonder what it feels like to have no mobile phone or no hair straighteners for a week," and then before you know it, they're off.

Fair play to them, even if they go right back to their usual luxuries of life, like a daily vanilla Frappuccino with caramel at Starbucks. At least they have demonstrable examples of them expanding their horizons and trying to experience more than their posh upbringing gave them.

If you travel, you see, hear, smell and taste things, then you come back and you can share that experience and spend that cultural capital in a way that makes you sound like the most clued up person on Earth. But there's a caveat:

In order to really expand your horizons to the maximum degree, or see things from the point of view of the local people wherever you go, you should really try to live like the local people. My trip to Madrid in 2015 is a great example of how not to live like the people in the place that you're visiting.

On a warm evening in March 2015, I landed at Adolfo Madrid-Barajas Airport around 9.14pm. By the time I got to the hotel it was past 10pm. I was starving and the best option I could think of was to order food from the hotel restaurant. What was funny was that I asked the waiter in the hotel restaurant to recommend the best dishes on the menu, but ignoring his recommendations I ended up ordering a burger and chips... And some Spanish apple juice to wash it down.

The next day, I was set on immersing myself in the culture in Madrid so I went to a local food market. It was so colourful; there was so much choice, and at decent prices whenever I enquired. Yet, my instincts told me to find out what a Spanish Chicken Royale from Burger King tasted like, so I did. I can confirm that it tastes exactly the same as a Chicken Royale in the UK.

Luckily, I then spent the rest of the day with my ex-colleague who was actually from Madrid. He gave me a true tour of the city and what it had to offer, which salvaged my holiday. Although, I should also mention that the next day, when I got hungry in my hotel room, I ended up calling the equivalent of Domino's, Duomo's, to try out a Spanish pizza.

I can laugh at myself for that lacklustre attempt at embracing culture, but the sad thing is many people do exactly the same thing and see no issue with it.

Do I think there's a problem with only going on holidays when half of the neighbourhood is also going? Yes, I think there's no way you will gather as much information about a new place if you spend all your time talking to the exact same people and basically doing the exact same things that you do at home. Okay, you got to ride a quad-bike or wear some floral patterned swimwear, but that's it.

Last, but by no means least, travelling usually provides great opportunities for you to challenge yourself in ways you either can't or just won't when you're at home in your comfort zone. Try out something new; whether you're great or crap at it doesn't matter, the point is to try out something new with the aim of pushing yourself. It doesn't even necessarily have to be something completely new. There's something about the short-lived nature of a holiday that provides good grounds to be extra ambitious with the goals you set.

The biggest, most glaring difference in the holidays I generally took versus those that my colleagues all seemed to love mostly fell into this category of holiday. A great example of one is a ski-holiday. For most people, there's always room for improvement on the slopes, and many others are pretty ropey when they get out there, but the fact that they do get out there, year on year, and challenge themselves time after time, proves something. Even if it doesn't prove very much, at least with their frequent trips they look and sound like someone who's living their best life!

Which of the following are you most likely to do in the next year?

Watch a rugby game 3.8%
Visit another town in the UK......19.6%
Go Skiing 5%
Travel abroad 71.6%

This might be a tricky thing to persuade you of, at least it will be if I go by the results of my survey, which said that more people were likely to quit their jobs in the next 12 months than go skiing. I asked over 100 respondents:

Interestingly, all but one of the respondents who chose skiing were of white ethnicity. I say this is interesting because it supports a generalisation that I imagine many people make: only rich white people go skiing. I don't believe this is the case, but it's not a million miles away from the truth either. Regardless, I think more people from BAME backgrounds will embrace skiing over time.

This isn't a debate about whether or not travelling is a good thing to do; rather, I'm saying that it's a great thing when you travel with intention. Whether you want to book a holiday to recharge, take some time off and really experience what it's like to live in another part of the world, or simply just to raise the excitement levels in your life and challenge yourself, there are plenty of options for you. Exclusivity is a real thing and classism does exist all around the world, but that shouldn't stop you from exploring and understanding the world more.

Cool, now you've got the all important context around why you should consider travelling more, here's some information about places you might want to visit:

INFORMATION

Breaks to recharge – UK destinations

Let's work off the basis that you want somewhere to recharge and don't have any issue staying in this country to do so. Let's also assume that you know that recharging and sleeping all day are not the same thing; you can still be active and recharge. On this kind of break, you should get loads of time to clear your thoughts whilst getting lots of fresh air.

The Cotswolds: on a good day with minimal traffic it could take you as little as two hours in the car from central London to get to one of the much loved (and hyped) villages in the Cotswolds, central England. Via train, you'd probably be best travelling up to central stations like Oxford or Bath and then making your way to one of the Cotswold villages from there. The place I always hear people mention is Bourton-On-The-Water, and Burford is another town that a colleague recommended I visit.

With all the hustle and bustle we are used to in London, as soon as you arrive you'll notice an obvious change in the pace of life out there. To get a real understanding of why these places are so prized, you should really spend a fair amount of time outside, taking walks on the public footpaths (there are lots of official walking routes online). You'll see a whole load of nice looking cottages and buildings made from old stone, a real change from what we see in big cities like London.

Royal Leamington Spa: this is a town in the county of Warwickshire, West Midlands renowned for its mineral water. If you've ever been to Coventry before, you'll probably have spotted a road sign with directions to Royal Leamington Spa as it's super close. However, while it might be geographically close to Coventry, it's got a notably different reputation as a place where the wealthy reside.

Royal Leamington Spa provides a nice

visual mix of old and new. I thought the town was surprisingly vibrant but still relatively peaceful in comparison to London. The buildings in the town centre are mostly Victorian or Georgian. Most are white or cream coloured, and the majority of areas appear to be pretty clean. A nice break away here would probably consist of booking a place on the outskirts of the town centre and then heading inwards for some nice food and things to do.

Stratford-upon-Avon: another good-looking, good-living town that's again not far from Coventry is Stratford-upon-Avon. A drive around the town will give you an appreciation of the general atmosphere, but many people love this town simply because it's where William Shakespeare was born and lived. If you're a creative type, this might be a cool place to get inspired whilst topping up on some all-important rest and recovery. Stratford-upon-Avon is by no means a huge town, but don't let that deceive you into thinking there isn't enough to keep you busy over a weekend or so.

Lake or Peak District: I would hear people mention both of these places all the time around the office, and I had little to no idea why they mattered or what was different about them. FYI: I studied history instead of geography at GCSE level, so that's my excuse. The Peak District is in central England and is like a little sibling to the Lake District up north; both have similar features but are truly unique places, and perfect if you like open spaces.

You'd probably be driving out to see them, and make sure your camera is super-sharp because the views are pretty epic – definitely IG worthy! Whether you get a little cottage out there or stick to a hostel or bed and breakfast, you'll likely not be far from some sheep and very large fields of green.

Sandbanks: if you're heading down to the south coast, you'll reach Bournemouth; keep going a little longer and you'll get to Sandbanks, one of the freshest parts of the UK. Sandbanks is the place for you if you want to be inspired and experience life in a truly affluent environment — there are some amazing residential properties out there.

The big thing about Sandbanks and the surrounding areas is, unsurprisingly, the sandy beaches (a bit of a rarity in the UK). People who live in Sandbanks are usually pretty well-to-do so you'll be rubbing shoulders with a few self-made Brits out there. Don't forget your wallet if you're heading out to Sandbanks and definitely see if you can get involved in the wide variety of things to do, like hire out a jet ski. You shouldn't be disappointed by the range of choice when it comes to places to go out and grab a nice meal, either.

York: another recommended location to visit for some peace and quiet and a more relaxing pace of life is York. One of our country's most historical patches of land, York is a great place to move about on your ten toes and learn as you travel. If you have an appreciation for architecture, you'll like York. No town has a bigger stretch of walls still intact from the Middle Ages, when they were built to protect the city, and today the city walls are recognised as a notable ancient monument.

Breaks for a completely new experience

For these types of breaks, it helps to be able and willing to take off a good couple of days, ideally a full week at the minimum, to really get the full dose of your new environment. I'd almost go as far as saying that these types of trips shouldn't even be called a 'break' at all, because quite often they entail more work than we might be used to in our usual environments. Often it's the case that flying out there costs a fair amount but once you're out there things aren't that pricey. This is certainly the case with most countries within South or Central America, Southeast Asia, and Africa.

It will be impossible not to make comparisons between what you're used to and what you're currently experiencing, it's just human nature. It's also human nature to gain an appreciation of the things you have when you are

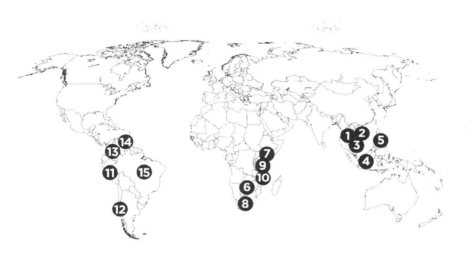

Hotspots across **Southeast Asia**	Hotspots in **Africa**	Hotspots across **Latin America**
1. Thailand	**6.** Botswana	**11.** Peru
2. Vietnam	**7.** Kenya	**12.** Chile
3. Cambodia	**8.** South Africa	**13.** Colombia
4. Indonesia	**9.** Tanzania	**14.** Venezuela
5. Philippines	**10.** Mozambique	**15.** Brazil

exposed to life without them, and that's what's really great about this type of trip.

The funny thing is that, quite often, these kinds of trips surprise people the most, as their experience is more positive than they expect. The media is partly to blame for this because it constantly portrays certain places through a negative lens, yet first-hand experience can prove otherwise. Respect usually goes a long way on these trips, whether it's respect for the local community, or their customs and practices.

Breaks to challenge yourself

To be fair, there are all sorts of breaks that may fall under this category but, as implied earlier in this book, a ski holiday is my favourite example of a break that forces you to step out of your comfort zone. As well as skiing, you could also consider trekking, climbing, or surfing experiences.

But back to skiing and why it can be a nice holiday once or maybe twice a year, if you've got the bread. First of all, you can get out on the slopes, get competitive and get better over time at a thrilling activity.

Like most people from anywhere in England, my general idea of a good holiday would be heading out to somewhere with more sun than we get at home, and the surprising reality is that, if you time your ski holiday right, you'll probably get a fair amount of it.

There are quite a few things to consider when lining up a ski holiday, so I've been asking some of my trusty go-to's about the key things to note. Here's what they told me:

- *Decide on a resort and when to go.*

- *One of the things you'll want is a decent amount of time out on the slopes, learning and improving. Certain times of the year will offer you more hours out on the slopes than others, but that usually comes at an increased price.*

- *When you are looking into which ski resort to visit you should compare things like lift prices and the costs of borrowing equipment if you're not bringing your own stuff. Prices of equipment can vary quite a bit depending on where you ski.*

● *It's like golf, if you think you might keep going out there, then it might make sense to buy your own equipment. Be sure to put your safety first and ensure that you get good-fitting boots.*

● *When you're out there, you'll realise pretty quickly how comfortable you are on the slopes, and the general premise is that the better you are the steeper the slopes you can ski down.*

● *Check reviews to see if the resort is favoured as a good place for beginners to ski. Hopefully, this should decrease the chance of any unnecessary injuries.*

On the topic of unnecessary injuries, take as long as you need to build your confidence and make sure you have travel insurance in case of any painful injuries resulting from falls.

Aside from that, it's pretty much just the usual things to consider when you're booking a holiday:

● Securing accommodation, taking into consideration hotels, chalets, shared accommodation, and distance to the airport.

● What else is there to do? Other activities like swimming or ice skating may be on the cards. What are all of the *après-ski* options at the resort? What's the nightlife like? Where are the closest places to shop, eat or drink?

Hotspots:

▶ Courchevel (France), Lausanne (Switzerland), Kronplatz (Italy), Alpbach (Austria), Verbier (Switzerland), Les Arcs (France).

Bonus Section

Finally, I thought I'd just throw out some other popular destinations you're likely to hear your colleagues mention at some point....

► Reykjanes peninsula, Blue Lagoon (Iceland)
► Mykonos (Greece)
► Lake Como (Italy)
► Ibiza (Spain)
► Monaco (French Riviera)
► Cong (Ireland)
► Bruges (Belgium)
► Budapest (Hungary)

Chapter Three – Art

Use your common sense(s)

If you asked me "What's a fine piece of art?" my natural answer might be something like:

"*Thank Me Later*, Drake's first full-length studio album, which debuted in 2010. It's a complete body of work, with the perfect amount of variety from track to track and relatable lyrics from verse to verse that keep me engaged from start to finish."

Some people would be able to relate to my answer and even agree; some people would disagree and point to some of the tracks they dislike on the album; others wouldn't count any rap album as a piece of art, full stop. That's not necessarily a problem. One of the main things we should all hopefully agree on is that art is subjective, meaning that my opinion and yours might not line up, yet we can each be right.

I like the idea of art being a form of communication and expression, a whole different language unique to the artist and his or her audience. The beauty of art is that it comes in so many different forms, be it music, painting, film or photography, the list is long and forever growing.

The issue (in the context of this book) lies in the fact that art usually goes hand in hand with classism and exclusivity. If someone told me this a few years a ago, I would have thought, "Who cares?" but some recent experiences have made me change my tune. My advice today would still be to embrace the art you <u>want</u> to embrace, but don't be closed to new forms.

One of the things that I'm big on is buying great gifts for my family at Christmas and on birthdays. Of course, it's all relative, so my idea of great and your idea of great might not line up, but the point is that I try to get gifts that I truly think the recipient will appreciate. January 2018 was no different; I took the hit and surprised my sister with two Grand Circle tickets to watch Dreamgirls at the Savoy Theatre.

My original intention at the time I bought them was to give the tickets to her and her fiancé, or maybe even one of her friends. However, because of the high price of the tickets, I decided that I would join her and recoup some of the cash loss. Also, I was conscious of the fact that, at age 26, I was yet to watch a musical at the theatre.

Right up to the day of the show, I had little to no expectations for the evening, but it took only about two minutes for me to be sucked into the plot and my final verdict was that the show was epic! As soon as it finished, I jumped on Twitter to let my 35 followers know how good it was, but Stormzy, who was also in attendance (and probably in even better seats) beat me to it.

When the show reached the halfway point and the lights came back on, the entire audience was already clapping and seemed as satisfied as I was, but then something strange hit me... Almost every cast member was black and, in stark contrast, almost every person in the audience was white. Make what you will of that, but I definitely wasn't buying that it was mere coincidence.

Audience Agency[4], a not-for-profit organisation that consult across England and Wales, analysed data collected by over 276 different art organisations and published some pretty conclusive results on this topic. Their 2016 study showed that, "Black and Asian people were underrepresented arts audience members at a national level."

A real mix of arts organisations contributed to their survey with museums making up the largest proportion (34%), but data was also collected from art galleries, performing arts venues such as theatres, and more.

By contrast, the British Film Institute[5] published some findings on cinema attendees across the country between 2003-2015 and highlighted that, "Black and minority ethnic groups (Asian, Chinese, mixed and others) were over-represented among the cinema audience."

Art is no different to many things in this world, in that enjoying it often comes at a price. Most of the time (but not always) you have to 'pay to play', and that tends to dictate what we choose to consume. If I go to the theatre to watch a play and it turns out to be pony, that would probably burn my chest more than if I ended up watching a bad movie at the cinema, simply due to the difference in ticket price.

In my survey on hobbies and interests, I included a multi-answer question which looked into people's preferred ways to consume art (see results on the next page).

Hopefully you weren't expecting any major shocks or thrills here either; a clear majority of respondents favoured watching things online, followed by taking trips to the cinema. Cost surely isn't the defining reason

What is your favourite medium for consuming art?

Cinema 51%
Museums 25%
Galleries 32%
Online (e.g. Netflix, YouTube or Socials) 68%
Theatre 35%
Concerts 32%

here? Or maybe it is, but I wonder if it's widely known that there are a number of free or inexpensive museums around the capital, and discounts for young people to attend plays at some theatres.

I think it's fair to say that it's not always about the money, and more to do with the fact that we make pre-assessments about art forms, just as we do about other things, and decide if we think we'd like them without actually looking into them at all. We use our memory bank of associations and connotations to help us decide if something is or isn't for us.

The important thing is really to isolate the reason why you're perhaps a massive cinema-goer but never visit the theatre, or why you spend hours every day admiring images on Instagram but never think to visit a local gallery and consume art in person. Have you weighed up the options and picked your preferred way to consume or showcase your art, or have you got to where you are today entirely unintentionally?

In another life, I would have the time to conduct research on the correlation between black people embracing art and October, a.k.a. black history month. I don't know if it's just me but I definitely notice a spike in people's appreciation of different art forms when October comes around.

Whilst it's great that people are taking notice of the amazing pieces of work being produced by black people, why do we only give them such attention in October? I doubt these creative individuals are hibernating for eleven months straight and only showcasing their work for 31 days a year.

In order to appreciate different forms of art, we may be required to draw upon different senses, be it sight, sound, taste, smell, or touch. Whether you have all of these senses intact or not, you shouldn't be stopped from consuming art in a variety of forms... Only you can stop you. I stopped myself by choosing not to try out the theatre for so long. As I said before, art is subjective but some forms are more easily or readily consumed by certain types of people.

You're probably aware of the phrase "use your common sense". Whether you've used it yourself, or it's been said to you (sorry to hear that!), the general idea is that you should draw upon a base of knowledge that is possessed by a lot of people. Whilst I get the general idea, the danger of this phrase arises when it is extended to refer to areas of knowledge that might not be as 'common' as some people think.

Some would say that it's common sense to not sit in front of a screen for too many hours in a day. However, in a world where we take a break from scrolling down our Instagram 'Explore' pages by checking what's happening on Twitter, and then catch up with friends on FaceTime straight after that, this piece of 'common sense' is arguably no longer so common.

To give credit where it's due, social media has definitely helped in some ways to spread the work of aspiring artists to wider audiences. Creative geniuses of all kinds are using their social platforms to get their work out there and are rightly getting the recognition they deserve as a result. So the future is definitely bright when it comes to people expressing themselves through art, but we need to be conscious of promoting more diverse art mediums.

Now let's explore some of the potential areas of common ground for art appreciation...

INFORMATION

Arts participation

You may already be in tune with your artistic side and the importance of sharing it with the world, but in case you're not, here's why I think you should be! I'm of the opinion that we all have an art form that we have the potential to be great at, but we definitely don't all choose to use it or develop it further.

If you're thinking about something and want to share your message with an audience, get creative and showcase your visual art!

Maybe you've got an idea of how to create something that could be nice for people to own; in which case, get making and showcase your applied art!

Or it might be that you like to perform and want to showcase your ability in front of an audience; whether live or recorded, get going and perform your heart out!

Nowadays, there are so many classes around; this can give you a way to connect with professionals and others with a similar interest, and there are even online tutorials to help you get started. But it's really up to you to ignite your talent and then nurture it. There are also group meet-up sites like meetup.com that can help you get more involved with others pretty quickly.

Photography:

Go beyond your bathroom selfie or Snapchats of the old man that's always snoring on your train. Living in the moment is so important, but sometimes capturing a moment can be equally as valuable.

Photography skills help people capture the moments they hope never to forget and it's hard to put a true price on this. Depending on what you prefer to shoot, photography can be a good reason to get out and meet new people or discover new places. Get the best camera you can afford and start right away!

Painting:

(Here, I'm talking about painting a picture on canvas, not a trip to B&Q to do up your front room kind of painting!)

There are so many popular phrases related to the act of painting. "Don't paint us all with the same brush," "Let me paint you the picture," or "a single picture can paint a thousand words." A painting is arguably one of the most powerful ways to get your message across and draw your audience's attention to a theme that you think is important.

Equally, though, painting is a great way to simply air out your thoughts; these might not be clear-cut, but you can leave the interpretation to you audience. There's no right or wrong with painting, which is one of the great things about it.

I don't think you have to pay big bucks to air out your thoughts either. Shops like The Works sell fairly inexpensive paints and canvases or thick paper that can enable you to get moving with it.

Sculpting:

Can you think of a better way to turn a whole load of mess into something with meaning? Sculpture is not your average hobby and I imagine few people were born with a burning passion for it but it's nonetheless a decent art form.

I'm throwing this into the mix because it's something a bit different, seems relatively pain-free, and is also a likely kudos-winner! Simple. Give it a try and see if you like it or if you're any good. If you haven't come across sculpting before, perhaps watch the old Lionel Richie, 'Hello' video sometime.

This is also a relatively wallet-friendly art form, and Amazon is your friend if you're looking to get started sooner rather than later, from the comfort of your own home.

If you'd prefer to indulge in the messy nature of sculpting outside of your house, then there are workshops and classes where you can do so. Again, have a look at sites like meetup.com or search online.

Arts Consumption

It's no secret that, as a society, we've become slaves to technology. It adds efficiency and ease to our lives for sure, but stay woke to the threat of technology turning you into a lazy sod! Before 'Netflix and chill', there was 'ask your mum for a tenner and go on a date to the cinema', but to many of us today the thought of consuming art outside of our houses, or worse, away from our personal devices, is a scary one, or a long-distant memory.

I get it, it's easy to get sucked into consuming everything from the comfort of your own home when you get to "watch now," immediately "watch the next episode," and then "watch more," but see if you can make it a thing to also consume media outside of your home or the cinema.

Theatre:

A newfound favourite on my list of to-dos is to visit the theatre. It's a nice way to both relax and be entertained by some real, raw talent. Of course, there's nothing wrong with a trip to the cinema but an evening at the theatre might be a nice alternative for those times when you want to treat yourself of someone you care about. Ticket prices vary quite significantly depending on where you choose to sit.

It will be hard to not appreciate the natural talent of the cast members once you're enjoying a good play or musical, and the great thing is that this is usually a given with any play you'll watch at a theatre.

There are a number of schemes out there to reduce the cost of theatre tickets for people, with discounted rates for certain age groups (usually 26 and under). However, if club 26 has sadly now passed you by, there are almost always ticket offers available via discount sites.

Museums:

You might know of some of the most famous art museums around the world, but how many can you say you've visited?

There's almost certainly a museum out there that caters to your tastes and interests, no matter what they might be. This is one of the reasons why people from all walks of life come out to admire art and culture at museums. You can take yourself through the collections that the museum has to offer and engage in intelligent conversation with those around you. Museums are also a great way to sharpen up your knowledge on a subject area, so you're learning in a varied way.

Art Galleries:

If you want to put your money where your mouth is and really show your appreciation for the arts, you might want to try visiting a gallery. Even if you don't want to actually put your money on the table by purchasing some artwork, it's still worth heading out to a gallery to discover new artists and their work. You know how at the beginning of this chapter I said that art is subjective? Well an art gallery is a place where you can really see that play out in reality. What's the famous quote? "One man's trash is another man's treasure"...

After reading this chapter, I want you to think about the ways you currently embrace and consume art and see if there's space to for more forms. A small step could be as simple as broadening the genres of music that you're open to listening to, or looking out for reviews from bloggers about their tastes and experiences.

Chapter Four – Hobbies & Interests

Your precious time

How does the saying go? "Show me your friends and I will tell you who you are." You'll probably come to appreciate that saying as you get older, if it doesn't already ring true to you. But arguably an even more interesting and effective way to get an idea of the kind of person someone is, is by examining the way they use their time.

You might wonder why we need to dedicate a chapter's worth of space and time to the subject of using time more wisely, but trust me, it's crucial stuff. It's also easily forgotten and under-appreciated stuff.

I'm sorry, but not really sorry, to remind you that our time on earth isn't endless, so it's crucial that we make the most of life's most precious commodity. You're going to need to allocate some of it for sleeping or resting, and then also some of it to things you might not want to do. That's practically a given. The question is: do you allocate enough time to things that you genuinely want to do?

Sunday evenings on social media are always funny because the comments about how painful Monday morning is going to be start flowing in.

"Ah, why do I have to go back to that place?"

"I can't deal with my colleagues speaking to me tomorrow."

"Can it be Friday already?"

Don't worry, you're not alone. There are probably way more victims of Sunday night/Monday morning blues than the number of people who liked your post, suffering in silence and dreading the pain that every Monday morning brings.

If, like me, you actually enjoy what you do for a living, you should count yourself as one of the lucky ones. The reality is, whether we enjoy it or not, work usually takes up a big chunk of our time every week, but it pays us back in one way or another.

The bigger question here is: how do you allocate your free time, i.e. the time in which you can do whatever you want to do? It's somewhat contradictory to moan about work because it's 'so boring' or 'so draining' and then purposefully not do anything to counteract that feeling in your free time.

It's just like when babies scream at the top of their lungs for a particular toy or random object. When you eventually hand it to them, they realise that they have no idea how to use it and lose interest in the item they'd been screaming for in little to no time at all.

Granted, when you're already shattered, the thought of doing something else that's not strictly necessary sometimes just seems like more effort. That's why you need to proactively decide what you want to do with your time and, importantly, home in on the things that you're genuinely interested in. What it is exactly that you commit yourself to doesn't

matter so much as the intention itself.

It's funny how people who are genuinely really busy somehow still make time for their hobbies and extracurricular activities, right? It's something I've noticed, but if you don't believe me, go online and read up on the people you'd classify as 'successful'. The key is to treat time as the valuable commodity it is, and stop using the lack of it as an excuse.

Once you're in control of your time, you'll find

yourself in the position where you're better placed to lend it out to others. One of my work colleagues who lives a pretty busy life recently started to give up an hour of his time each week to help out at a homeless shelter not too far from his home. He took an interest in the backstory of a homeless man who he'd seen on his commute to work, and now he has a new use for his time.

Acknowledging your interests and hobbies by setting aside some time to dedicate to them says more about you then you might think:

● It tells people that you care about your wellbeing and health, whether that's physical or mental

● It indicates that you appreciate the importance of time and you're not wasteful

● It demonstrates that you have a life outside of work and you're passionate about your pursuits

A hobby or interest outside of work is a great symbol of your commitment to your wellbeing above all else. But most people recognise that free time can be a gift or a curse, depending on how you use it.

I'm a strong believer in choice, and in most circumstances you have one. You've made a choice to read my book (thank you!). As a result, you'll hopefully make some other choices after digesting the messages of the book, and so on and so forth. Well, that's the plan anyway.

On the other hand, you can think about the fact that we don't *have* to do anything. I said it myself, "we all have a choice," right? Regardless of whether or not it feels like it, even getting out of bed on a Monday morning is a choice. How we spend our leisure time and the things we call our hobbies are pretty important choices because they directly affect our mental, physical, and social wellbeing. If you're like me, you can pick up new hobbies really quickly but drop them even faster (this isn't necessarily a bad thing). Some will stick and some won't, but you'll be in a better position to make a call on whether something is for you or not once you've tried it.

I asked the following multi-answer question as part of my survey in order to get a better idea of the things people presently like to do in their free time:

If the 102 responses to this question are anything to go by, it seems that meeting up with friends is currently pretty high up on the list of priorities for the weekend.

What type of activities do you usually get up to over the weekend?

Play sport 33%
Meet friends 90.2%
Travel 45.1%
Retail Shopping 40.2%
Other 18%

That's all well and good, but try to take the lead on the plan for the next meet-up, and see if you can steer it toward some mutually beneficial things to do or see.

Your extracurricular activities shouldn't be a chore or something that you are prone to neglect. Remember, you are not your job, nor are you your corporate title. I don't care how much you love you work, try to distinguish between actual-you and work-you. Don't be one of those people who get asked in an interview "so, tell me about yourself," and have nothing to say because your life revolves entirely around your job and sleep. Or even worse, around someone else's hobbies and interests.

On the subject of interests… You might already be interested in politics — or, maybe you're not. If you're not, let me guess, it's because politics just isn't interesting, you don't know anything about it, you don't trust or like politicians, or you just don't see the point in bothering when your voice is never going to be heard?

There's a good chance that I can relate to your line of thinking, but I'd rather put that to the side for the purpose of our development. Instead, I'd rather highlight why it's important to at least keep an ear to the ground when it comes to politics.

The most obvious reason is that it affects our livelihoods, whether we like it or not. It's far better to be in the know, irrespective of your personal opinions, and by simply keeping up to date with affairs you can become a helpful resource to your loved ones, friends and peers, which is always a plus.

Here, like most parts of this book, it's again about attitude and being open-minded enough to make it work for you. Whether you dedicate some time every day/week/month for a roundup of current affairs is up to you.

I personally had to make some proactive changes in order to stay in the loop with the latest happenings. To start with, I downloaded a couple of news apps and opted-in to the live updates features from most of them.

I watch Question Time most Thursday nights for a weekly round-up of the topical issues having the greatest effect on our country. It might even be as simple as listening to a podcast in the morning as you get dressed, or signing up to a news platform.

Politics is just one aspect of current affairs that creeps into a lot of conversations in the corporate world. I'm not saying that all of a sudden you're going to discover and unleash some newfound passionate commitment to one of the political parties or become an MP groupie, but you can begin to make more informed decisions on a daily basis and help those around you to do so too.

On a different note, but also related to how we spend our free time, it's always impressive to hear that someone is "learning" to do something. Often, what that something is doesn't even matter, just the fact that you are driven enough to focus on learning something outside of your work commitments gives a positive impression of your character. It positions you as someone who has a goal to reach, someone who isn't afraid to challenge themselves, and someone who's not a time-waster.

I know a guy who always talks about how inefficient we can be as humans; to really hammer the point home, he translates the little instances of wasted time from seconds per day into minutes a month, and then hours or days per year. On the other side, the little steps we take toward bettering ourselves also add up over time, so what you can squeeze in over the weekend or in the evening *does* matter. To put this into practice, here's a list of things that people have actually told me they are learning to do:

INFORMATION

I'm learning how to...

Fly – it took me a little time to believe the person who told me they were learning to fly a plane, because their 9-5 had literally no link to aviation. However, he mentioned that flying had always been his passion as a child and how his realisation that we "only live once" got him to sign up to flight school. To be fair, your hobbies and your work don't have to align, so I should never have doubted him.

Taste wine – this person turned a simple hobby of enjoying an occasional drink with friends and family into a skill that serves her and her guests well. She's tried more wine than I could ever name, travelled to vineyards across the world, studied toward a professional wine tasting qualification, and built up a valuable collection of bottles... All in a pretty short space of time.

Speak in a new language – when my friend told me he's going back to the classroom to study Spanish, I nearly spat my drink out. But he's not lying, he's enrolled at evening school to crack on with his long-term goal of being able to speak Spanish fluently. Managing evening school and a full-time job won't be easy, but he's super charged up and has his eyes on the prize. I told him when he's done he should learn Yoruba next!

Value art – I couldn't tell you this person's motives here, whether it's to make money from flipping art or to start a collection of his favourite pieces, but either way it's a skill that I'm sure will be a valuable one to possess. So far, his interest has led to him reading up on how to evaluate art and attending art fairs and museums to build up his knowledge and sniff out any potential purchases.

Salsa – Weekday evening classes have turned an explorative new hobby into a full-blown passion for one of my friends. We met up after not seeing each other in person for about nine months and straight away I knew something was up! She looked so fresh and full of life, I had to ask what the secret was... Salsa!

Play the guitar – this person never struck me as someone who was particularly musically talented, and there was a valid reason for this... she wasn't! She had no musical background beyond her primary school endeavours but her fresh perspective on living life to the fullest led to her taking up new challenges in different aspects of her life, one of which was to learn guitar.

Or why not see if there's scope to switch it up...

Sometimes it's not even about picking up something completely new, as, granted, this might sound like too much of a mission. It could be as simple as adding a bit of variety to your current hobbies and interests. Identify the things you're currently into and see if there are any variations that might support your growth by broadening your horizons and overall subject knowledge. I'll run you through some examples of how this might work in reality:

If spending time with your friends is your thing, then why not suggest doing something new while your at it like taking a short trip out to somewhere that you haven't visited in the country. Or trying out one of the local restaurants wherever you go as opposed to the chains you always visit.

You might enjoy keeping fit and regularly use the treadmill at your local gym, but how about also signing up to your local running club or getting involved with an organised run which allows you to raise money for a cause you believe in.

Your hobbies, your interests, your time. Don't be overly dependent on everyone else's motives without actually dedicating time to what you personally enjoy doing! Be the most well rounded, interesting and open you!

Chapter Five – Fine Dining

Expensive Taste

Apparently, the difference between "eating"and "fine dining" is that eating simply meets the basic need for survival, whereas fine dining also satisfies the mind, body and soul... Well, that's what the waiter at a high-end restaurant told me after I told him I was writing this book.

When I think of fine dining, I think of fancy silverware and spotless white tablecloths. Of refined décor and super formal service from the waiting staff. Whilst these things are present in some higher end restaurants, they are not a always a given in all fine dining restaurants today.

Most people expect to experience fine dining at one point or another, be it for birthday celebrations, date nights and other romantic celebrations, or as part of their business activities. Fine dining is a 'nice to do' that I didn't know was indulged in so regularly by anyone with less than a million pounds in their bank account. That was before I stepped into the corporate world. The reality is, fine dining is a pretty stable fixture in the diaries of many of my peers in the corporate world and something that you might benefit from some specific information on.

In some respects, I'm also writing to the old me because it wasn't so long ago that I would be the first to say no to suggestions of a pricey meal and instead always default to a cheeky half-chicken with two sides. I still do this, of course, but now I also treat myself and those around me where possible.

The motivations for fine dining will vary. Some see it as an experience that goes far beyond the food you eat, and for others each bite, and each specific flavour tasted, carry serious weight. Some people use fine dining as a way to impress someone and/or get them on their side, and others simply go to say they've been, or to be seen.

Something that's definitely a positive when it comes to fine dining in London is that there are loads of places to try out. With respect to food, London is definitely a strong contender for the title of "city of the world," and the most open-minding city of them all!

A sure way to pick out the best of the bunch and the most worthy contenders for your time and money would be to leverage the efforts of the ever-growing community of food bloggers, or "foodies", that is out there. It pays to follow these folk on your socials and check out their reviews on the best places to go and then what to order when you get there. Beware, though, these people will pepper your timeline with seriously good looking food at all hours of the day.

They say that birds of the same feather flock together, and it seems that this applies to gourmet restaurants. If you want the crème de la crème of swanky eating in London, then location is a fairly good give away – your Mayfair, Chelsea, Hyde Park, Knightsbridge and Notting Hill-based restaurants are good places to start.

An even surer way to differentiate between the best of the bunch would be to check online to see how many Michelin stars the restaurant has got. This basically means how highly rated the restaurant is by a bunch of critics that no one even knows. There are a good number of London-based restaurants with Michelin stars denoting their worthiness.

In order to get a feel for the restaurants that people currently favour I chucked the following simple question into the survey:

Where is your favourite place to eat?

Nando's was favourited more than
any other restaurant
(Named 8 times)

Whilst the responses were very mixed in terms of favoured cuisines, a clear overarching trend was that casual dining restaurants were preferred over fine dining restaurants. However, some people didn't specify a restaurant and instead highlighted a type of cuisine — Thai and Chinese being the most popular.

The fact that casual dining restaurants were, on the whole, preferred over more lavish restaurants could simply be down to coincidence, or potentially a consequence of the barriers to entry when it comes to fine dining, i.e. the high prices.

It's definitely not recommended to get into debt in the pursuit of expensive food and wine, but you could see if there's a way to enjoy fine dining at a cost that's comfortable for you. Look out to see if the restaurant has a set menu, as these usually offer good value for money relative to choosing each course from the 'a la carte' menu. If not, you could skip the starter/entrée, or perhaps pass on dessert. The lunch menu is typically lower priced than the evening menu, so it might make sense to go out for a nice lunch as opposed to a fancy dinner.

Also, sites like OpenTable, Quandoo, and Virgin Experience Days all regularly post deals and limited offers from a wide range of fine dining restaurants.

If you're willing to occasionally accept the higher prices and open up to fine dining some more, here's an important heads-up:

Be open and willing to adjust the way in which you judge what makes a good dining experience.

This isn't to say that all of a sudden your taste buds will transform once you start dining in higher end establishments more frequently. It comes down to something that I noticed pretty quickly when I was out with some of my peers.

You see, when you're a non-fussy, creature of habit like I am, the deciding factors in whether or not a meal is worth the price boil down to a couple of straightforward considerations:

1. Did the meal taste nice?

2. Am I full as a result?

3. How bad was the damage (cost) in relation to my level of fullness?

If I was being super picky, I might question the level of spice and how chewy/tender the food was… So really not that fussy at all.

As you step up a level in the world of food critique, 'nice' doesn't cut it any longer; diners expect food to taste 'exquisite'. Who cares if it only occupies a tiny section of the plate, or if you leave the restaurant feeling lighter than when you came in. When considering their eating experience, fine dining customers ask themselves questions like:

1. Did the meal taste like it was prepared with the right level of delicacy, and was it served to perfection?

2. Did the atmosphere tie in nicely with the tastes and flavours of the meal?

3. Was the service exemplary in terms of speed and the subject knowledge of the waiting staff?

If a restaurant counts itself as a fine dining establishment, it will be aware of this criteria and understand that it has an obligation to provide a pleasurable experience for its guests. Your needs become their priority and your feedback is usually very valuable. They must ensure that what they are offering could not be experienced for a fraction of the price elsewhere.

Believe it or not, it doesn't actually stop there. The sensei of fine dining aren't too concerned about the portions being generous, neither are they satisfied with the food tasting exquisite. This group of diners prioritise the finer details about what exactly is on the plate above all; they want to know exactly where the food was sourced.

They seek to taste exclusivity in every bite and want the full rundown of exactly how the food landed on their plate. From which country? In which field? From which farmer? These kind of restaurants hire 'experts', not waiting staff, so feel free to ask them questions about the menu and benefit from their knowledge. If your grasp of wine options isn't too strong, the sommelier will be your best friend.

I'm sure you know this already, but spending big bucks in a restaurant definitely doesn't guarantee that the dining experience will be enjoyed. It really depends on what you look for in a great dining experience and, as I just detailed, different crowds look out for different things. If you're hosting the meal, make sure you do your homework on the restaurant prior to arrival. Hopefully, that will prevent any unwanted surprises and unnecessary disappointment.

The key is to adapt to your surroundings. Fine dining restaurants will all try to put their own stamp on the experience they offer to justify the prices they charge. Be flexible and manage your expectations when it comes to things like portion sizes; don't expect apples to fall when you shake a lemon tree!

I came into the corporate game with the dining etiquette of a 'Man vs Food' contestant, so it was a pretty steep learning curve getting to grips with certain things. Fine dining is part and parcel of some roles within the corporate world, particularly client-facing roles, but it pays to have an idea of the rules of the road, irrespective of your position at work.

Dining etiquette is best acquired through practice, but below are a a few tips that might be useful. Hopefully, they will serve you well when you're next seated at a fine dining table.

INFORMATION

First, there is in fact method behind the cutlery madness:

● Only certain foods require specific pieces of cutlery that aren't already set out when you are seated, e.g. steak knives, lobster forks and crackers.

● You start by using the cutlery that's farthest on the outside and work your way inward as you move through each course.

● The cutlery on the outside is usually slightly smaller in size, so that's another indication that this is the cutlery that should be used for your starter.

● Dessert cutlery is usually placed above your plate.

● Don't scoop food up with your fork, the pointed edges or 'tines' of the fork should

be facing downward in almost all circumstances.

- Dare I say it, avoid eating your chicken with your hands at any point.

Don't forget your napkin:

- Once you're seated, remember to unfold your napkin and place across your lap.

- Dab your mouth with your napkin, don't rub it all around your mouth.

- You should place the napkin on the left side of your the plate when you've finished eating.

- If you need to get up for any reason during the meal, asked to be excused and place your napkin on the seat.

Chop responsibly:

● A complimentary basket of bread usually comes before you've even ordered. Use
the small bread plate that's beside your
starter plate.

● It's correct to tear your bread with your
fingers and then butter/olive oil each piece
with your bread knife whilst you eat.

● Try to make sure everyone on the table has
been served their food before you dig into
yours... I said "try".

● Try not to sit there blowing your food at
the table. If it's too hot, converse with your
guests and wait until it cools down to a more
manageable temperature.

● Refrain from updating your IG/Twitter/
Facebook/Snapchat followers with pictures
of your meal as you eat.

Other bits of information:

● It's pretty standard to order some sort of caffeine-based drink after the meal (as a dessert replacement, with dessert, or after dessert).

● Phones off the table (but you knew this already), and elbows too.

● If you burp, fart or spit some of your food out by accident, leave the vicinity immediately... just joking!

● If you're unsure of something, look at the person who seems to have the most experience of fine dining and copy them. Yeah, I said it!

"Keep calm and carry on eating" is the moral of this chapter. See how many of the useful tips you're already familiar with and try to get to grips with the new pieces of information. Dining experiences are meant to be comfortable and enjoyable, so have fun and enjoy your meal!

Concluding Message:

Focus on what you can control.

Act with intention.

Be open, always.

Seek new information and share it.

At the start of this book, I let you in on a particular unpleasant thought that I had that just wouldn't go away. Going to university and mixing with a lot of people from fairly privileged backgrounds made me wonder… Would the corporate world be a tough world to live in, not being accustomed to many of the things that seemed to be second nature to my peers?

The thought still creeps up on me, and I imagine it may creep into your own mind at one point or another, but there's no need to panic. There's always merit in taking action by plugging any gaps in your knowledge that you identify. The point of this book is to demonstrate that you can take control through reading up on things, asking questions, or simply getting out there and learning from experience.

Differences in tastes, hobbies and interests will inevitably arise from diverse upbringings and personal experiences, but the key is being open and embracing these differences. Take an interest in more than what you might be accustomed to; it may turn out to be beneficial, and might set the tone amongst your peers to return the gesture and embrace the things you like.

The best thing you and I can do to level up the playing field isn't the same as what organisations or educational institutions can do. The best thing you and I can do is focus on the things that we can control. There are certain parts of the social/cultural inclusion equation that are within our control, and others that are not.

Focus on the things that you can realistically have some effect on: how open and willing you are to enriching yourself; how willing you are to demonstrate that you are the multi-faceted, open-minded, and embracing person that you want your colleagues to be. Those are the most important bits of information that under-lie the content of this book.

You'd have the right to question my authenticity as a Brit if I didn't make any reference to the weather in this book, and I can't have that, so here's a concluding thought:

How many times have you made plans to go out somewhere, got dressed and then opened the front door to see that its raining heavily outside? You're determined to follow through on your plans but you've now got the reality of bad weather to deal with.

You could choose to stay at home, maybe wait until it stops; you could sack your plans off all together, or you can grab an umbrella and press on with whatever you've planned to do.

When it comes to diversity and social inclusion, focusing on what you can control is equivalent to grab-bing your umbrella and pressing on. It might not solve the wider issues of unfair prejudice, social exclusion, and discriminatory behaviour but it's an important part of the equation and a big step toward creating the envi-ronment we are all hoping for.

Let's keep it one hundred: some of the differences in social tastes and interests are a result of generational imbalances in society. So, yes, there are longstanding differences, but *"Rome wasn't built in a day"*. Focus on leading by example when it comes to being open to understanding new things.

When my dad made the decision to move to the UK, he moved with the view of making things easier for the wife and children he would one day have. We're here now, and things are probably easier than they would have been if he hadn't had that vision, but is that it?

Is this the maximum level of success that was tied to that vision? I don't think so. I think there's more to it, and it will take working smart to progress further from here. It's going to require meeting some very clear challenges and overcoming some not so clear obstacles.

People always go on about the importance of working hard, and it's obviously important, but it also pays to know that working smart is at the very least equally as crucial. Working hard will hopefully get you to your desired destination, but working smart is all about getting there through an efficient use of your time and energy.

Don't expend all of your effort in a professional role and forget to nurture your personal development. That's not working smart. Working smart is being open to new experiences that can support your physical, mental and social wellbeing alongside your committed efforts at work.

Seeking to understand and appreciate more than what you may have been exposed to previously is key to harnessing new relationships in the corporate world. Ignorance isn't always bliss. In fact, in this context I would argue that ignorance is the complete opposite of bliss. Acquiring new information and applying what is relevant and beneficial to you is more likely to get you closer to a state of bliss.

This isn't an excuse to brown-nose your peers, but taking an interest in some of the areas mentioned will most likely help you connect and nurture meaningful relationships with more people. There's immeasurable value in that alone. Recently, I saw someone post on LinkedIn that "We are as valuable as our network."

We've covered sports, travel, arts and culture, hobbies, interests and finally, fine dining, but you might uncover other areas of difference that make you wonder. That's fine, the same principles apply, focus on what you can control. Focus on not turning a blind eye to things you're not naturally accustomed to. Ask yourself: what's in it for me? Can this better me in any way? Is this something that can potentially open up other doors for me later down the line?

The truth is, the answer to these questions probably won't be clear right away, so there will be an element of second-guessing things, stepping out of your comfort zone, and going with your gut feeling. I fully appreciate that price will play a big part in your decision to explore some of the things mentioned in this book. As nice as it would be to walk outside and pluck fresh £50s off of a tree, that's obviously not the kind of world we live in.

Of the different areas flagged, think about what matters most to you, or what interests you most. Weigh up the different ways to make things possible for you. Starting small is always a good option if money is the main barrier. Without sounding like too much of a cliché, an investment in yourself is arguably the best investment you can make. Use the information I've shared in this book. Interpret and manipulate it in whatever way you have to, to pursue self-improvement.

If you value what you've read, feel free to spread the word. Make sure that you don't get caught out in the fallacy of holding onto information that could be useful to others, trying to keep it for yourself. Bring others in wherever possible; the more inclusive, the better.

Diversity and inclusion are the buzzwords on the lips of many corporations and educational institutions. That's great, because it means more people will get the shot that they deserve, but you shouldn't get complacent. Be bold and be open to the idea of broadening your horizons and your perspective. Don't imprison yourself within the social constructs of what you're 'supposed' to know, like and appreciate. Remember, there's always room to improve, room to learn, and room for more experiences that can support and enhance your wellbeing. Focusing on what you can control will give you power and direction in your journey toward a more level playing field.

Notes

[1]Smith, A. (2012). *Luck: What It Means And Why It Matters.* Retrieved from https://books.google.co.uk/books?id=ppENYCgTWeAC&pg=PA3&source=kp_read_button&redir_esc=y

[2]Office for National Statistics: 2011 Census. *Population of England and Wales, Ethnicity facts and figures*
https://www.ethnicity-facts-figures.service.gov.uk/british-population/national-and-regional-populations/population-of-england-and-wales/latest

[3]Department for Transport: *2013-2017 Travel by distance, trips, type of transport and purpose, Ethnicity facts and figures*
https://www.ethnicity-facts-figures.service.gov.uk/culture-and-community/transport/travel-by-distance-trips-type-of-transport-and-purpose/latest

[4]The Audience Agency. (2016). *Data to Measure Diversity*
https://www.theaudienceagency.org/insight/data-to-measure-diversity

[5]British Film Institute Research and Statistics. (2016). *Audiences*

https://www.bfi.org.uk/sites/bfi.org.uk/ files/downloads/bfi-statistical-yearbook-audienc- es-2015-2016-08-25.pdf